Heights and Depths

Heights *and* Depths

George Hobson

FOREWORD BY
Maria Apichella

RESOURCE *Publications* · Eugene, Oregon

HEIGHTS AND DEPTHS

Copyright © 2021 George Hobson. All rights reserved. Except for brief quotations in critical publications or reviews, no part of this book may be reproduced in any manner without prior written permission from the publisher. Write: Permissions, Wipf and Stock Publishers, 199 W. 8th Ave., Suite 3, Eugene, OR 97401.

Resource Publications
An Imprint of Wipf and Stock Publishers
199 W. 8th Ave., Suite 3
Eugene, OR 97401

www.wipfandstock.com

PAPERBACK ISBN: 978-1-7252-8972-7
HARDCOVER ISBN: 978-1-7252-8968-0
EBOOK ISBN: 978-1-7252-8971-0

03/10/21

Contents

Foreword by Maria Apichella | vii

Part I

Embroidery | 3
Flight | 6
Black | 7
In the Killing Hours | 9
Moon Over Rwanda | 11
Afghan Woman | 14

Part II

The Gift of this Long Day | 21
Conceit | 26
Fragments | 27
Despond | 28
Heights and Depths | 30
Questions | 31
Temptation | 33
Envy | 34
Deliverance | 35
The Garden | 36
He is not a Sea-Going Man | 38
Speak, Mirror | 46

CONTENTS

Part III

Morning on the Brittany Coast | 51
After Rain | 53
Sun-Patch | 54
The Copper Pan | 56
The Sea of Night | 57
Forms | 59
Signs of Love | 60

Part IV

The Dream | 65
French | 67
Fire on Riot Hill | 70
Today | 76
Butterfly | 80
Memory, You are Cruel | 83
A Prayer | 84
The Bell | 86

Part V

The Stallion | 89
Night-Hawk | 91
A Vision | 93
Her Dear Face | 94
Mouse | 95
Scribbles | 96

Foreword

I AM A POET today because of George Hobson. In the 1980s, the Hobsons befriended my family. My father worked at Radio Oxford, George was studying for his doctorate in theology, and I was a child under their feet. Like my father, George was an artist, an American far from home. Through being a part of their friendship, I learned that making things, be it a poem, a painting, a good meal, a well-timed joke, or even a relationship, is what God designed us to do.

When I was eight, I remember popping into George and Victoria's apartment with my mother one afternoon. George was arranging his photographs in preparation for an exhibition. His living room was filled with A3 sized photos propped up along the sofa, on chairs, and all over the carpet like an unfinished mosaic. I remember being drawn to an image of a luminous glass bowl on a stone ledge. George moved the pictures around, comparing the nuances of color and content, seeking a narrative. He was totally absorbed. I realized that this is what artists do: they create beauty from a muddle. But, because we are only *like* God, and cannot simply think or breathe something into being, we must grapple with it. There is a practical side to creating art. It involves time-arranging and re-arranging, making decisions and backtracking, being interrupted, taking coffee breaks, phone calls, and coming back to try again. Eventually, George published some of these images alongside his poetry in *Rumours of Hope*.

When I was fifteen, George and Victoria had returned to Paris but were still present in our lives. George would send manuscripts of poetry to my father for feedback. I used to sneak the poems up to my room, lie on my stomach, and read them. Some of those poems are here in *Heights and Depths*, including my favorite: "Signs of Love." This poem taught me about the power of repetition, simile, but also that God calls out to us through the physical world. This poem captivated me; I fell in love both with God and poetry.

> Stars, you are like crystals frosted
> On night's window-pane—
> And you burn and do not melt:
> Signs of love,
> You burn and do not melt.
>
> You are like sparks frozen
> On the fireback of night—
> And you flame and do not die:
> Signs of love,
> You flame and do not die.
>
> You are like mica flakes
> In night's granitic wall—
> And you glint and do not dim:
> Signs of love,
> You glint and do not dim.

The words I read in these exciting manuscripts were portals into George's world: a world filled with stars, sun patches flickering along stone walls, a copper pan hanging low like an autumn moon, a kitchen mouse peeking out of a hole with hope in its bright black eyes. George's writing is specific and sensory. I saw, smelt, and tasted what he saw, smelt, and tasted: dewy gardens, purple plums, umber fields, grey goats, the sound of bells, and rain.

> After weeks of dryness,
> It rained all night.
> Morning woke up soaked and shook itself like a wet dog.
> Sun came on stage like an Italian tenor
> And sang a love aria to earth.

FOREWORD

Earth blushed.
Rumpled clouds, exhausted, shambled off to the west.
Chunks of blue sky lay in puddles on the roads, gleaming.
Diamonds glittered in the fields.

Yet these are not escapist poems. George has travelled the world to pray with those who suffered trauma, and his poems, in this book and in earlier collections, look at evil with eyes wide open: the genocides in Rwanda and Armenia, and, going further back in time, the horror of slave ships. I found the violent images utterly shocking when I read them all those years ago. George's poetry shows the world for what it is. However, in the manner of a modern John Donne, he also writes about his own inner battles, doubts, and frustrations. Like the Psalmists, George cries out to God. Life is good, but it is fragmented and filled with anguish.

> My God, will you not put the pieces of my soul
> Together? Will you not fit my jigsaw years
> Into a whole? A puzzle I accept to be,
> But as a lively pattern, with integrity.
> How can I, pelted by the rain of tears
> That battered my beginnings, find my role,
> When all is under mud?

George's openness before God and his readers, his striking use of language, and his ability to capture stories compelled me to write poetry with as much wonder and grit as I could muster at fifteen. I carefully included all the five senses, followed similar structures, and expressed my own lyric prayers. I remember my father smiling at the obvious Hobson influence. *That's how writers get started*, dad said. *By copying their mentors.*

My family lived from hand to mouth when I grew up, but it was because of George and Victoria that we got to travel. They often invited us to stay in their stone house in France for the summer holidays. They always welcomed us on the first night with a feast, and then drove off to Paris. They left the fridge and cupboards packed with brioche, brie, saucisson, and Orangina. By opening their home for us to explore, I discovered the world of beauty. Their house was full of nooks and crannies. I remember seeing objects from his poems such as the copper pan, and the very same glass bowl from the photograph years ago. I heard the bells, smelled the goats, and tasted the plums. I also snooped through their bookshelves. This is how I discovered the work of T. S. Eliot, Emily Dickinson, Czesław Miłosz, and Michael O'Siadhail—all influences on George's work and therefore mine.

When I was twenty-five, I caught the train from Aberystwyth to Oxford because he was in town speaking at a conference. It was January, I was half-way through my Ph.D. in creative writing, and I was stuck in a poetic rut. This time I was the one bearing a manuscript, and it was a mess. I wanted his opinion, but I also just wanted to see George. I was hollowed-out from a complicated relationship back in Wales. Going on a pilgrimage to see the Hobsons when facing a crisis was an Apichella tradition. Thankfully, they were never fazed by us, and they always fed us before getting to grips with the problem. This is what George did yet again. He took me to a deli, bought me a coronation chicken baguette, a bottle of water, and we ambled back to the church. We sat in the cold vestry with our coats on and ate. Then we spent a few hours talking about my work: things that were good, things to develop, and things to cut. George always took me seriously and encouraged me. My scrappy manuscript ended up becoming *Psalmody*, and it was shortlisted for the Forward Prize in 2017. After we talked poetry, I told George all my relationship troubles and we prayed. George is a serious poet but also a kind, wise, and compassionate minister. This shines through in his work. He is a poet-priest who knows what it is to love radically, through sacrifice and self-giving.

> In you, Savior, I meet the Other;
> I meet my friends, my most dear wife,
> Enemies, the wounded. You smother
> Anxious, bleating self. You give life,
> Lord. Yours. It's *your* life you offer.

I took the train back to Wales inspired and focused.

FOREWORD

Throughout each season of life, George has demonstrated that recognizing beauty in all things, and the conscious act of creating, are two sure ways to know, share, and celebrate God. I did not learn this from a textbook or a sermon. I learned it from conversations overheard in childhood between George and my father, seeing him persist at his photography and poetry, and through the love he has shown and shows towards my family, others in need, and to his wife Victoria—who deserves to be recognized here. She is more than a background muse. If it were not for Victoria, George would not be the man he is. In my memory, she was always razor-sharp, classically beautiful, charming as a film-star, generous as a grandmamma, and witty as a New-Yorker columnist. I have had the privilege of knowing the Hobsons personally, hearing their stories, staying in their house, eating their food, reading their books, and receiving their prayerful wisdom. Through reading this book, I hope you may do the same, vicariously. These poems crystallize all I have learned from George. And maybe you too will be compelled to create your own works of art—whatever form that takes. After all, it is what we are meant to do in the limited time we have on earth.

Maria Apichella
Author of *Psalmody* and *Paga*
mapichella.com

Part I

Embroidery

Surf embroiders the ocean's hem,
Waves criss-cross athwart the rocks,
Weave froth-skeins,
Stitch sea to land with threads of foam.
The sky scowls, dour.
Oh, sour the age, sour our hearts!
Sea growls,
Rollers pound the sand,
Gull-cries flay the air.
Out at sea scattered breakers foam;
Beach-grass shivers in the breeze blowing landward;
The brown dunes brood.

Thus our anguished souls, our age.
Thoughts run to and fro,
Cross, criss-cross;
Memories break over the mind,
Churn,
Swirl in linking arcs of foam.
Hopes swell, fall;
Fears curl like cobras;
Despair hisses.
Flotsam surfaces, bits of self,
Fragments sunken under time,
Borne by great waters.
On the shore the heart shakes, troubled.
The ocean stretches out,

EMBROIDERY

Back,
Beyond the beginning;
The sky stretches up,
Out,
Beyond the end.
This is what was and what will be.
The wind blows landward off the ocean,
The roots of the beach-grass grip the sand fiercely.
The waves boom on the beach and run up the strand,
Hissing.

Thus our time.
Cultures criss-cross, clash.
There is a heaving,
A weaving;
Then a crack,
A breaking,
Tumult—
Down crash the combers.

In time's folds are embroidered countless beings;
We too are stitched there,
In Love's embroidery.

> *Beyond the beginning, God;*
> *Beyond the end, God*

The wind comes in hard off the sea,
The beach-grass shakes;

EMBROIDERY

But in the wrack and wreck of time,
We are held.
We are God's memories,
Preserved in his Word,
Promised a future.
Though we forget who we are,
Or do not wish to know who we are,
We are not forgotten,
By grace we are remembered.
We can hear,
We can cry out,
We can choose to live.
Hung betwixt sea and sky,
Shuddering in time's wind,
We are sustained.
Now, here,
A voice may speak out of that wind
And strengthen our weak knees.

Let us lift up our hearts and give thanks

Flight

The trees in the wind are wild,
The crazed leaves roll and rock,
Their shadows jig in the sunlight
On the brown earth of summer's close.
Leaves gone yellow strain,
Cling, yield finally, fall.
In myriads they scatter down blasted avenues
Like crowds fleeing cold-eyed militia
Under orders of some delusional tyrant.
Among them are those who have forfeited their place,
Who have broken ranks with the party line,
Who refuse what the reigning propaganda calls "fact",
Or else who just happened to be hanging out one day on their twigs
When a violent gale arose suddenly and carried them off.
In masses they race along the bloody thoroughfares
And scamper every which way
Until all are mowed down by the murderous wind
And settle in heaps on the sullen ground.

Black

It has been a long time since I was still.
The night has been a roaring—
For long it has not been that bowl of stars distilling silence
that I knew when young—
that image of peace.

Always now when I seek quiet in my heart
I hear only a roaring—
For in the enormous night I see galleons plying oceans,
piles of coal heaped up,
non-renewable persons.

Never can I know again in this life peace—
At night only a roaring,
blacks heaved overboard by thousands, blacks into black,
unshackling traders
from cumbersome cargo.

All is black; of all, blackest the hearts
of those traders. A horrible roaring
roils the sick ocean; millions murdered howl
in the valleys of waves,
weep on the mountains of water.

Blacks' white bones lie strewn in ocean's night—
In that awful deep, what a roaring!

BLACK

With shells and the skeletons of fish they lie on ocean's floor,
claimed by pure hearts—
mud's heart, God's heart.

I—man—stand doomed. I am undone.
In soul's night, a terrible roaring.
We humans are blackened, no health is in us. Diseased.
In Hell too, bones—not their bones.
In Hell too, memory.

Of such catastrophe, what can Christ make?
When he will come, upheaval—a roaring!
His blood saves, but the stone-hearted will be judged.
He will scour the sea
and raise its black bullion to life.

In the Killing Hours

In the killing hours, when demonized men
Armed with machetes hacked people to pieces
Under the palms and the pale eucalyptus
And groves of banana trees quaking, I hear
The nervous barks of dogs wracking the night,
Now howls, now baying moans, now yips and yelps;
And in my troubled sleep, restless like the leaves,
I know these are the mutterings of the dead.

When mercy fails, and hatred, that vulture,
Hunches on the hills, cold terror shakes
The body like a stick: stones bleed, iron sweats,
Fire freezes. Hearts turn red,
Like lobsters boiled in water. The soul shrinks.
Horror gouges out all eyes. The stars go blind.
Men turned to insects scuttle on floorboards,
"Cockroaches" squashed under stamping boots.

The Nyabarongo River runs red with corpses;
Bodies litter the valleys and hills, the roads,
The fields, hedges, marshes; heads and limbs,
Feet and torsos, are strewn through the towns,
In the gardens among the potatoes and beans,
In flower-beds next to the roses, in streets,
Houses, churches, hospitals, schools. Only
Grunts, cries, and moans are heard in the land.

IN THE KILLING HOURS

No monument can bring back the slaughtered.
Remember the faces and names of the children,
The women and men who perished in terror.
Their voices and laughter linger in sunlight
As it gilds flamboyants and gay bougainvillea
On the roads to Gitarama, Kibuye, Butare,
And the thousand green hills that stretch through Rwanda.
The birds cry their names at dawn and at dusk.

But the roll-call of songbirds will never give life
To the hundreds of thousands who died in that evil. Their
Plaints in the night will not cease. Vengeance is God's,
Not man's. The Redeemer remembers
Their names, for the day when he shows forth
His judgment. His mercy will raise them to life,
He'll catch out the wicked. Then the great beasts
Will roar, the hills leap, the trees gambol for joy.

Dogs howl in the night. The dogs yap and fret.
In the ground the bones of the wretched dead twitch.
The bamboos are shuddering. The banana leaves rasp.
Those who survived are asleep in their beds,
They toss and turn fitfully, grasping for hope.
The dogs cease their barking; an early cock crows;
Three others reply; a hoarse raven caws.
Now birds are piping. In the east day gleams.

Moon Over Rwanda

I

The huge moon lifts from the broad hill,
A great Leviathan breaching a sea swell.

Scraggly trees on the ridge top stand
Black on the bloom rising from the dark land.

Up into infinite night climbs
Moon. Its soft ode to sleeping earth rhymes

With crickets' chants, sheep's bleats, a dog's bark,
Harrumphs of frogs, lowing of cows—all hark

To moon's pale song, as Rwanda's soil,
Tough grass, shrubs, plants, ants, rest from toil.

II

Not all rest. Not the mother
Sweating in darkness, remembering the slaughter,

All her children, her children's children,
Her uncles, aunts, cousins, all her kin

And thousands more, thousands, slashed
And sliced, bellies ripped open, skulls smashed,

Their houses burnt, cattle killed,
Banana groves axed, bean-plots stomped, wells filled,

Filled with corpses, corpses and blood,
The soil sprouting bones, running red mud.

III

You feign shock, distress, you scowl
Gravely, self-importantly, then howl

With the God-mockers, the wolf-pack,
Who, there where men put men to the rack,

Scent "God" and track and murder him
To assuage their grim guilt. For on the slim

Edge of their souls, the fault, they know,
Lies with men such as they, lies with the low

Aims of bitter hearts like their own.
When one day awful death looms, and, alone,

They face dark, will they cry to the One
Whom, when the pain was other men's, they stoned

With scornful words? Will they cast pride
Down and see God's true face, once denied?

IV

Over the red land, the sad land,
Moon rises, soothes the mother's heart with hands

Of gold, speaks to her fierce grief
Solace, intimations of relief

Beyond imagining, the promise,
By Christ's deed, to lift men up from the abyss,

Give back to each his own true face,
Luminous, Love's handiwork of grace.

On fair Rwanda shines high moon
With comfortable words: "He comes soon."

Afghan Woman

Welcome

You smile—dawn rises—
Light flows from the rising corners of your mouth,
From your green eyes under their awnings of lashes,
Your eyes caverns,
Fires deep down glowing, light
Flowing out of dark deep down,
Out of sorrow's caves,
Like sun out of night, light
Flowing from the corners of your mouth,
Your mouth lifting like a curtain's corners,
Light pulling back your taut lips,
Sounding the music of your bare bold teeth
(One is missing),
The tambourines of daybreak,
White flashing, light
Flowing from your eyes like melody,
Melody from under the violence inflicted
The assaults
The scorn
The rejection
The cruelty beyond telling that you as woman have suffered.

For a moment you forget where you are
You forget you are safe
For a moment
You frown, grow sad, look down,

AFGHAN WOMAN

Then you remember—
You remember where you are
You remember we are here

You smile.

Hope—it is hope that pushes back the dark,
Hope like the sun breaking night's grip,
Hope rising in the violated heart,
In the body battered by demented men:

A howl that ricochets among the mountains,
Torrents gushing through raised locks,
Wind bursting out of canyons,
Steam erupting from beneath the earth

And now the words come.
We listen—
That is why we are here.
We listen:
Words,
At first slow,
One, two, a few
Words, one, two, three,
Words uttered furtively,
Uttered like steps along a passage where the floorboards creak—
Will one be heard?—
Word on word,
Slowly,

AFGHAN WOMAN

Fasterfaster
Syllables linking into words into sentences paragraphs
a flow now of lava-language pouring from the crater's mouth
thrust out by hope:
Out, the story of beatings/whippings/slashings—
hope the explosive;
Out, the tears/rage/cries for justice—
hope the catalyst;
Out, dreams, glimmerings, prospects for a future—
hope the fuel.

You sob,
Your tears stream,
We hug you and hug you.

At last you grow quiet.
You wipe away the tears.
You smile.

Do you know where you come from, woman?
It was *death*.
You were grain crushed between millstones,
Iron held over flames by a blacksmith's tongs,
A body nailed to a cross.
It was *death*.

AFGHAN WOMAN

But that is passing away—
You are being loved.
You have come out of your tent—
You are being seen and you see.
You have spoken
(Words are the woman)—
You are being heard.

Your wan lips part,
Light flows from your eyes.

You smile

Part II

The Gift of this Long Day

I

I've waited long for dawn to come.
At last the light flows bloody out of dark.
Life is always born in blood.

The sun pokes up from the womb of night,
Heaven's sign, day-bringing child:
The sheets of cloud are bloody from the birth.

I awake in many rooms, lodged like caves
In memory's pock-marked hills.
All night I've wrestled with the moon and stars,

Straining for clarity, for the patterns
Those clear bodies trace upon the void;
I've wrestled too with absences,

Eyes of heaven shuttered, pin-pricks
In the cosmic cape sewed up,
Hints of otherworldly brilliance gone.

The sun's birth saves me from this agony.
The rooms I wake in echo with the wild fits
Of a child not sure he's loved, of a lad

Plying space, of a man afloat in dark.
But now, by God's grace, this sear past
Has lost its strength to warp me.

Yet memories still ring as I awake,
Tolling on the hills. Does memory move the heart
By showing seed and flower in a single frame?

Does change itself make sad? Or is it time's
Sheer beam, bringing to view the blight
Upon our days and all our doings,

The fault imposed by past upon the present,
By present on the past, making even blessings
Doleful, already charged with loss?

II

I'm sad because our world is sad.
Lacking purchase on eternity,
It rattles, anorexic, in the wind,

Or wades, obese, down urban strips
Awash in words and gaudy scrawls,
Signs signifying nothing.

Astray in wilderness, facing a tomorrow
Made of particles and homogenized
Cheese, the world's got cabin fever.

THE GIFT OF THIS LONG DAY

The blight is on the cinder block
As well as on the rose. My memories
Bear the pain of flowers dried

And set beside a vision of their glory.
But in the downhill race of daily hours,
I'm burdened by another sorrow

Than the slow decay of special
Things once known and loved: I grieve
Our rejection of fidelity,

Of permanence. Ah, the great
Bell tolls for the whole wide earth,
Announcing desolation and dismay.

With no glimpse of glory, nor fear
Of hell, nor interest in our source
And end, we find the present heavy

Like a sack of rocks, loaded with guilt
We can't assuage, hungers we can't
Appease, rancor that saps our hearts.

Duration is a pointer to eternity,
No more; but we'll not know its depth
If all we make of history is data.

The sun's birth saves us out of cosmic night.
We can't redeem ourselves. The day will be
Our tomb if we should think it otherwise.

III

Age creeps up on us on padded paws;
The poplar's shadow pivots round the trunk,
Points across the darkening field of corn.

We have a long day's labor, then comes
Evening and a taking stock. Is this our end,
Or the end of our beginning? For whom

Have we shed blood? Whom have we served?
We deal out life a thousand ways,
Or deal out death. Give it or take it,

Life is in the blood. In the end,
Now, always, this we need to know:
In blood we're born, by blood we thrive,

Enhancing or reducing our planet's
Life. What value has our long day's
Living, our long day's slow dying?

THE GIFT OF THIS LONG DAY

IV

Day gutters in the west. The city's windows
Reflect its flame. The sky erupts
In glory to acclaim the sun, its king.

The city's towers never raise their heads.
Their rooftops rub indifferently
Against the sky. The sunlight gilds

Their surfaces but fails to pierce
Their tinted glass. They flaunt their bulbs,
Deny the sun the time of day—

Yet only by its mighty fire
Do their weak tubes glow white.
As evening falls with a burst of neon,

I think on time with wonder, on the gift
Of this long day, on coming night;
And I rejoice that gold Dawn soon will break.

Conceit

My life is like a metaphor that doesn't work,
An utterance containing terms that jar;
All God's ingenuity so far
Has not made sense of me: semantic quirk
Conjured in a lurch of creativity,
Bold trope that doesn't quite come off.
I'll not blame fate; my Author's God, who rough-
Drafts men and angels. I appear to be
A parody of poetry: weak-rhymed; with imagery
Lush but flawed, like clouds gross enough
To drown the plain—if they broke! Instead, they lurk
Aloft like futile armies waging war.
Here no triumph of rhetoric occurs;
One hardly knows to what the trope refers.

Fragments

My God, will you not put the pieces of my soul
Together? Will you not fit my jigsaw years
Into a whole? A puzzle I accept to be,
But as a lively pattern, with integrity.
How can I, pelted by the rain of tears
That battered my beginnings, find my role,
When all is under mud? My heart cracked then;
My blood, since, spurts fitfully among the shards.
O God, govern the divided federation
Of my mind! Make functional your reparation
For my own and my fathers' sins! Your gracious words,
Like garments, hang loose on my weak frame; my thin
Bones jut out like a starveling's; make haste,
O God, to save me from my sullen waste.

Despond

If I be not loved of God,
I must soon weary
Of the inconclusive gropings
And headstrong elopings
Of my unquiet mind.

For I am restless without God;
My mind's a tangle, dreary
As an urban sprawl; hoping
Eludes me, and power of coping:
Oh, may He loose my bind!

I paw heavily through snippets
Of the past, finger smoke-shreds
Of imagined futures: turning
Times like pages, learning
Nothing but more care.

Half-thoughts race like whippets
In my brain, or dig in beds
Of dying flowers, yearning
For resolution to the burning
Ache in me to share.

To share? A joke! Share what, pray?
Half-cooked ideas? Notions
Undisciplined and dull? Seemings

DESPOND

And appearings? The sordid teemings
Of disorderly emotion?

If I'm not loved of God, my way
Is dark: the fitful ocean
Of my mind must quench the gleamings
Of a port afar, the dreamings
Of a berth for my devotion.

But I know well I'm loved of God!
He knots the tag-ends of my days,
Lays hold the febrile straining,
The gray, wintry raining
In my heart, and brings release.

Oh, may He ever be my God!
He lifts me from the ways
Of futile care, gaining
Me ground for hope, deigning
In His love to root my peace.

Praise Him!

Heights and Depths

I've climbed many mountains through the years,
Not with ropes, spikes, crampons, just hands and feet.
I've hiked joyfully by peaks where rock wears
Year-round an ice-stiff winding sheet.
I've threaded canyons, crossed passes, clambered over
Scree to win bare wind-wracked summits
Where eagles soar and poised hawks hover
High in silence, beyond stone's limits.
Bleaker times, I've plumbed dark chasms, pits
Of terror, where clear sense shrivels, truth shrinks,
Tumbling rock-falls batter hope to bits.
Here, lost in night, the stricken heart sinks
Down, undone by fear. O Lord, you trusted me
To trust you in that void, you whom I cherished.
Beside me, though seeming far, you rallied me
To call to mind those heights—*or I had perished.*

Questions

The new moon is a comma.
But what, O God, is the sentence
Whose comma marks a pause?

The gibbous moon is a rugby ball.
What game, O God, are you playing with us
On the tractless field of night?

The full moon is a silver coin.
What treasure, O God, lies hidden
In the star-filled vault of heaven?

The aging moon is a boomerang,
Soon to be flung into the void
(Or perhaps it is an old bone
Waiting to be buried).
Will it curve back to us, O God?

Father, will you spell out a word again
On the black screen of our night?
Will you open our eyes to read?
(We have forgotten how to read.)

Will you cry "Play!" again
To the thrilling game of love
We used to play?
(We have grown cold,
Our limbs are numb.)

QUESTIONS

O God, will you shine again
In our vacancy?
Will you speak to us again
By your poet the moon,
And prophesy the Light of Life
Concealed beyond the stars?

May we be born again?

Temptation

Under silence, in the afternoon,
The curtain by the open door breathing
In the slight breeze, I confess my heart is prone
Sometimes to droop, I feel lonely, a seething
Of emotion roils inside me like a whirl
Of leaves flushed by wind, a rush of fears
Comes at me, a kind of anguish, a swirl
Of feelings, turgid, nameless, to neither years
Nor places linked by any obvious chain
Of reference, echoing no memories,
Summoning no grief in particular, a bane
To be repulsed—*for these are enemies!*
Enemies of life, of love, of things
Concrete and true, durable, with shape and structure.
So, to these vain, vagrant pityings
Of self, I will say "No!"—and end their torture.

Envy

When I consider my limitations,
The peaks I've glimpsed and never scaled, the things
Done, those—more—undone, recriminations
Puncture me, I grow flat, my mind clings
To what I'm not, forfeits myself. The heights
My imagination ogles cast queer
Shadows on my heart, marks of the grim flights
Envy sponsors beyond my native sphere.
This is but pride. Who am I to strain
For competencies other than my own?
Mine are fine. This bent to covet grain
In others' fields is folly. Seeds sown
Elsewhere yield no crops to feed my years.
Eyeing others' harvests reaps only tears.

Deliverance

Galaxies of blackthorn make long trails of smoke
Between the ploughed brown fields; explosions
Of forsythia spill gold stars on the oak-
Lined hills, proclaiming spring's combustions.
Out of winter I emerge like one kept
Hobbled in a cloister full of creaking
Doors and half-voiced plaints, where bright truth crept
Like a shadow on the cold walls, scarcely speaking.
I gulp great drafts of air in this wild spring
That breaks across the land in waves of fire;
This burst of stars, these lifting flames, sing
Loud songs of Exodus and heart's desire.
Now my dear earth soars up to heaven's spheres,
And God's erupting joy destroys my fears.

The Garden

A green canvas is my bed,
My frame a wide blue cloth
Embroidered with swabs of cotton.
Bands of gray and green surmount my grass:
One is like a wall chinked with moss and topped with ivy;
A second is dotted with dabs of purple paint
And puts me in mind of fruit trees;
A third is a chain of green flames
That look like heads of broccoli and evoke oaks.
My horizon is the distance hinted at by tones,
By keys of gray and green,
And, around it all,
By the blue cloth containing me and everything else.

Something like a wind blows through the canvas,
And the greens seem to rustle and converse.
The blue frame translates the language of light
And radiates an invisible reality.
I note flecks of brown among the cotton swabs
That evoke birds soaring and swooping,
But the flecks are only signs, they don't move.

As I lie here resting on the canvas,
I realize I too am a sign, no more,
A creature conjured by paint—
And yet a *peculiar* creature,
Distinguished by bold brush-strokes
And the bright yellow color the artist chose to create me.

THE GARDEN

I feel a glory in my flesh,
What I might call an *aspiration*.
On the green ground I glow like gold,
I stand out.
(I am speaking modestly—my conception isn't my doing!).
I remember that the artist spoke to me.
"You are Man," the artist said,
As he daubed the yellow on the green;
"You are my image,
Called to be a sign in my creation
Of the glory that is mine
From before the foundation of the world."

Remembering these words,
I rise from the canvas.
Suddenly all about me is movement.
Ripe plums drop from the fruit trees,
The green flames along the horizon dance,
The flecks in the cotton tufts begin to fly.
Now I myself stand tall and raise my arms
To the wide blue cloth containing me:
"Glory to you, O great Artist,
O great Creator of all things having being,
You who have painted me bright yellow like gold,
Who have given me dominion over all these signs of your glory,
I lift my head,
I lift my arms,
I lift my voice to praise your Name forever and forever!"

Amen!

He is not a Sea-Going Man

He is not a sea-going man.
Nothing but water in every direction
As far as the eye can see,
Frightens him,
Even in calm weather
When the sea is flat like a wood engraving.
Nothing but water everywhere
Is like Nothing, *point à la ligne.*
Nothing.
But even worse than the expanse of water in every direction
As far as the eye can see—
Even worse that the thought of himself being abandoned
And floating alone in the middle of the ocean—
Is the thought of the *deep*,
The thought of what's *under* the surface,
The deep going down into black,
Himself sinking down into black,
Sinking down
through
miles
of water
miles
and
miles
of water

Sightless
Soundless
No solid thing

Nothing

Only now
and now
and now
a sense of monstrous presences,
beings,
huge beings,
creatures,
shapes,
here,
there,
shapes,
dim shapes coming towards him:
Terror

No doubt about it,
The sea really frightens him:
The expanse of it, the deeps of it.
He is definitely not a seagoing man.

Nor does he scale mountains.
The sight of a climber glued to a rock-face
Appals him.
Emptiness

Man as a dot on a blank page.
Is the rock or the void more real?
Neither is real without the other, of course.
But for him,
The crannies and cracks that give the climber a handle on solidity
Are not enough:
The danger is too great,
The emptiness too numbing.
The momentary experience of exhilaration
At the overcoming of oblivion—
The experience of being beyond self
Even while experiencing self-mastery
By virtue of courage and technique and hard work—
Cannot, for him, at least as he imagines it,
Make up for the terror of the void
And the horror of dropping through space
And exploding on rocks a thousand feet below.

No, he is definitely not a mountain man,
Not a scaler of rock-faces.

He avoids neon-strips in congested megalopolises too,
Bright zones of colored signs
Blinking and beckoning,
Where everything is for sale
And herds of hopeless souls distract themselves.
Futility
Rouge and powder,
Masks,

HE IS NOT A SEA-GOING MAN

Squalor,
Hands that clutch,
Lips that lie,
Corruption,
Seduction,
Exploitation,
Filth.
This is Hades, where shades waver and quiver and strut and quake,
Each alone inside itself in the midst of the mass.
Here there is no rock with cracks and crannies,
No contact between persons,
Nothing solid,
Only shadows passing each other,
Forms of gray ash.
Yet he knows too—
And he knows that it is important to hold onto this—
That inside the ash
Some coals still burn,
Some hearts still beat.
He claims to have heard that God is at work among the neon signs,
Blowing on embers,
Opening eyes behind masks;
He claims to have heard that sometimes kind words are spoken here,
Sometimes merciful gestures are made.
But, for all that he knows this to be significant and not to be forgotten,
He can't deny that the emptiness of the neon world
Makes him feel like a man afloat in the middle of the ocean
Or a climber clinging to a sheer rock face:

He experiences *horror*.
No, he is definitely not a lover of neon.

And then there is night.
He is very scared of night.
No sight.
Absence
If there is sound,
It is like the *absence* of sound.
To the eye,
To the heart,
No solidity.
Things—what things?—are unjoined,
Or so it seems;
Their places cannot be found,
One does not know where they are
Or what they are.
At best there is groping.
He might touch something,
But it feels like nothing.
No names are here.
No sight, no sound,
No thing.
Utterness.
Our star is absent,
So *we* are absent.

He finds all this frightening.
It is like wading in emptiness.
He is definitely not a night person.

And, of course, like everyone else he is terrified of *pain*.
Here words fail him,
Even words like "Nothing" or "Absence".
He asks: "What can one really say about pain?"
There is physical pain,
There is mental pain.
With pain, the cup of emptiness is full:
Obliteration
Here we enter the abyss.
Torture is the worst,
Because hate inflicts it,
Not necessity:
One is alone in the cosmos,
Undergoing oblivion.

And here, suddenly, a cry erupts from his heart:
"God, I'm dying!
I'm all alone in empty space!
Do you hear me—I'm dying!
What am I supposed to do?
Hello—God—do you hear me?
Do something!"

As this cry wells up in him,
He remembers what a friend once told him about Jesus:

"Jesus was nailed to a cross," the friend had said.
"He hadn't done anything wrong.
It was for us.
Jesus actually *embraced* the abyss we simply suffer—
"For us."
Then the friend had added:
"And three days later Jesus was raised from the dead."

These words—the memory of these words—
Fall upon his heart like gentle rain.
Life
He trembles.
What is he to make of this?
Neither a sea-going man nor a climber nor a lover of neon,
He isn't a church-going man either.

But he feels deep calling unto deep.

"*My* deep," he mumbles.
"*My* abyss."

He feels life invading his dead night.

He muses:
"That means that even on the rock face,
Hope is present."
And then he remembers something else his friend had said:
"One of the names for Jesus is the *Rock*."

And here he feels his heart brimming
With something he could only call joy.
It is like a sunrise:
Light bursts forth inside him,
Inundating everything.
He breaks out laughing and crying all at once,
And all his terrors—
As when a flame sets a bundle of papers to burning—
Shrivel up and turn to ash.
And what is left,
As he looks around him,
Is *solid*:
Everything around him is *perfectly solid*.

Speak, Mirror

Speak, mirror.
Offer me mountain flowers
at ten o'clock in my morning.
Offer me handfuls of color in a speckled meadow
high above a lake where clouds flower
like the eyes of a forgotten face once loved.
My eyes in the mirror offer the flowers plucked
At ten and at noon,
at two, at four,
now at six,
now as light weakens,
as shadows blotch the Mont Sainte Victoire,
now as Cezanne sculpts with strong strokes one last time
the momentous mountain.
Mighty strokes delineating permanence:
this is rock—
no place here for flowers speckling youthful meadows.
Underneath the flowering and the wilting,
this stands.
Yet even rock grinds down:
of that which is forever, a sign only;
and now night is coming.
Oh, I welcome your handfuls of color, mirror;
and I welcome you too, great mountain;
and you, great artist, making your mountain present;
but under your remembered flowers,
pressed in my brief day's dog-eared album,
and under your rock accumulating shadows

and those great strokes seeking eternity,
offer me that which abides:
Rock of Ages.

And behold, you speak:
behind those eyes, mirror, I see heaven's bloom reflected;
behind that mountain, one greater;
behind that painter, the Creator;
behind my face, Christ's face framed.

Part III

Morning on the Brittany Coast

Blackbirds hop on the dew-wet grass,
A horse whinnies in a saffron field;
White-hulled boats, striking out from harbor,
Rock on the swell of the morning sea.

Seagulls bustle in the wake of a launch,
Settling and swaying on the jostling ripples;
The shadows of magpies dart flapping
Across a meadow edged with Queen Anne's lace.

A copse of tangled privet shrubbery
Flecks a path with brown mosaics;
Buttery broom and blackberry bushes
Conjure hawk moths, honey bees, horseflies.

Mottled butterflies settle on gorse
Now long past its golden flowering;
Thread-like antennae quiver an instant,
Then wings flutter up from the thorns.

Sailing instructors gather their charges
In parallel groups of green-striped dinghies;
Lining them up on the stippled water,
They teach the youngsters to play with the wind.

The cries of sailors over the water
Mix with the piping of birds in the briars;

MORNING ON THE BRITTANY COAST

The purring putter of motorboats merges
With the wash of the tide on the strand.

Sailboat buoys, white, yellow, pink,
Stud the wide bay like party balloons;
Glued to their double on the water's surface,
They bob on the rolling wake of sloops.

The fiery sun scales the mountain of sky,
Shedding its heat on ocean and land:
Textures of summer on the ancient seacoast,
Woven by the Master Weaver's hand.

After Rain

After weeks of dryness,
It rained all night.
Morning woke up soaked and shook itself like a wet dog.
Sun came on stage like an Italian tenor
And sang a love aria to earth.
Earth blushed.
Rumpled clouds, exhausted, shambled off to the west.
Chunks of blue sky lay in puddles on the roads, gleaming.
Diamonds glittered in the fields.
Among the grasses, flies danced;
In the soil, worms inched.
Oaks caught breezes and clapped their leaves.
On air's loom shuttling warblers wove invisible fabrics.
From under hedges snails appeared, savouring wetness;
They gathered in groups on the grass and gossiped.
On the brambles lining the muddy paths
Bright berries, like miniature dirigibles, floated,
Each pregnant with a raindrop.
Will the babies bring more rain?

Sun-Patch

Sun-patch quilted on the kitchen floor
By happy mediation of a window-pane:
It lies on mundane tiles, a semaphore,
Signaling an awesome, sweet refrain.

Noiselessly it slides across the tiles,
Swatch of tissue from the realm of Day;
Rides, bright sail, by scented isles
Of grapes and peaches on the lacquered tray.

Round the basket hanging from the beam,
Round the hempen ropes, it folds from day
To day, at the appointed hour, its pliant gleam,
Weightless, impalpable; and goes its way.

On the table, smoothed by centuries of hands,
It sets a comb of honey on the whorls;
Later, luminous on stone, the sun-patch stands
Trembling, alive to voices in the walls.

Now it bandages a broken chair, now stains
A chest; upon the objects in its path it plays,
For each in turn, a proper melody: strains
Otherwise unheard, of beauty and of praise.

SUN-PATCH

To the kindling in the hearth it puts a flame; shines
Copper pot and ladle; streaks white
The blackened fire-back. Then suddenly the vines
Outside the window stir with wind, the light

Appears to shake, to flap its golden wings
As if to flee into the blue. Just seems:
The patch still sails beyond the shadow, sings
Still beyond our human being and our dreams.

See now: defying gravity, it gilds the stair
And bends around the wooden rail; unfurled
Again on stone, it melts away in air.

The Copper Pan

The copper pan hanging from a nail above
The hearth, gleams. The pan is sunk in stillness.
On its curved edge reflected fingers
Of flame play scales. A two-pronged fork,
A copper ladle hanging near the pan,
A spatula, a spoon, a perforated
Chestnut roaster, streak the mirror of its face
With golds and browns, the hues of setting suns,
Light's greasepaint. Made up, opulent, the pan
Sits on air, a harvest moon emblazoning
The blackened chimney. In the silence it plays
The harmonics of stillness. My quickened
Ear picks up the notes above the flames.
The ancient sphinx, sunk in sand and night,
Echoing the music of the glittering stars,
Is no more strange to the inquiring heart
Than this round pan hanging from its nail.

The Sea of Night

On the sea of night,
As if borne on an invisible ship,
The young moon sat on a deck chair.
She faced East;
Currents, hidden, carried her westward,
But she wasn't bothered.
The West could wait.
For now she was happy just to sail among the stars.

The view from the deck chair was splendid.
A big blue ball afloat in the Void caught her attention.
It glittered with artificial galaxies.
She wondered if angels lived there.
But then she thought no,
Angels live in starlight
(She'd learned that somehow),
And the light on the blue ball wasn't like starlight.

High above where she sat on her deck chair
A suspension bridge made of silk spanned the sea of night.
She wondered what worlds it connected.
Far off she saw Andromeda,
An old friend.
"Andromeda never seems to age," she thought to herself.
"I'd like to be like her,
To live forever,
To live forever with the angels and the other stars."

Just then a cloud crossed the bow of her ship.
She felt a pressure in her back,
Like a great sorrow.
Then the cloud passed.
Again she was riding high on the sea of night,
Facing East,
Enjoying the view.

Forms

In darkness is no form. "Let there be light,"
Spoke God. Form was close behind:
Earth, sea, living things—God's delight.
Matter gave God's Word substance, line
Drew forth shape. Color lent to forms
Divine emotion. All things cohered,
Having one Source, the Breath of God. Norms
Provided structure, so that what appeared
Could unfold freely, in harmony,
Each creature in its place and bound
To every other, making perfect melody,
A cosmic symphony of luminous sound.
That music, the Word's joy, plays in light:
God's love ringing out, confounding night.

Signs of Love

Stars, you are like crystals frosted
On night's window-pane—
And you burn and do not melt:
Signs of love,
You burn and do not melt.

You are like sparks frozen
On the fireback of night—
And you flame and do not die:
Signs of love,
You flame and do not die.

You are like mica flakes
In night's granitic wall—
And you glint and do not dim:
Signs of love,
You glint and do not dim.

You are like points on the sky's
Flat graph, charting darkness—
And you beam and do not go out:
Signs of love,
You beam and do not go out.

You are like barnacles
Fixed to night's black vault—
And you grip and do not let go:

Signs of love,
You grip and do not let go.

You are hot balls of fire
Hurtling through Dark's cold—
And you glow and are renewed:
Signs of love,
You glow and are renewed.

You are like sentries standing
At the outposts of space—
And you watch and do not tire:
Guardians of love,
You watch and do not tire.

You are like pangs of desire
Aching in men's souls—
And you burn and are not quenched:
Hunger of love,
You burn and are not quenched.

God's bright tongues
Speaking to mortal men:
Language of love,
You call and do not cease,
You call and do not cease.

O bright stars,
Image of holiness,

You are pinholes in the shroud
That hoods our world—
Behind you is Original Light,
Love Himself,
Beauty,
To Whom all signs point:
And He is Day
In Whom is no darkness at all:

And He is Day
In Whom is no darkness at all

Part IV

The Dream

When you are old, when you count
On crooked fingers
Your days left in this world,
When your toes, like roots,
Cling to the patch of earth under you,
Then you'll dream another time,
Couple with the wind again,
Run slender fingers through the hair
Of ageless loves,
A breeze riffling the trailing stems
Of willows.
You rose early,
Sang with the sun;
Gracefully you touched your cheek to day,
Lifted your head in laughter;
You conceived years to come numberlessly,
As rabbits breed in the field,
As fish multiply in the sea.
But the years will have turned to days,
And the days houred,
And the hours tip-toed into oblivion:
What once moved will be fixed,
What was to be done will have been done.
The time you'll dream will be as distant
As is now the moment of that dreaming;
Behind you, like chaff in a swathe
That's cut and gathered,
Will lie scattered the countless days

THE DREAM

You now conceive to come.
The dream you'll dream will be familiar,
A shadow on the ground
Pivoted half-round under you,
Your shadow on the still ground.

French

It was long ago I learned French.
A *pension* in Lausanne,
A house with a garden,
Ten European students, one American,
1957-58.
The Algerian War was raging.
De Gaulle came to power that spring.

I was seventeen,
A bud just opening.
I didn't know the name of my flower.
French watered me.
It was a stream flowing in a dappled forest.
Its vowels were pools, its diphthongs eddies,
Its consonants stones in the stream-bed.
In shadow French was sensual,
In sunlight it glittered.
Its "r", as in "rêche", was a growl in a cave;
Its "on", as in "thon", was a snail in its shell;
Its é, as in "doré", was a bird's sharp peck;
Its "ui", as in "nuit", was a kiss,
Night's sweet air,
Musk,
The woods' scents.
Words were marjoram, cinnamon, clove.
Their euphony was mulled wine.
French was an embrace,
It was lovers mating.

FRENCH

Its beauty rooted me in ages and beyond ages.
Here was the infoliated rose.
It made me ache for the ultimate bloom of being.
And here was Monique.
Her skin was ivory, her hair, night.
Her face was the moon.
She spoke the French of Valéry through lips like plumbs.
To hear her speaking it, I trembled.
To her brother she uttered the liquid vocables of Portuguese,
Her native tongue.
She ravished me.

And here were her counterparts from the north:
Antja, a German beauty made of earth,
With hair like a wheat crop;
And buttercup Cooky from the Netherlands,
With her bright porcelain smile.

I was young and didn't know about women,
And all these scented flowers troubled me;
I was like a bee entering a garden.

And so,
Black and blond,
Dark and light,
Night and day
Staked out discordant claims in my soul.
It was mellifluous French with its intimations of unity
That preserved my spirit.

FRENCH

It bore me on its flow upward towards transcendence,
Where the sensual and the rigorous,
The erotic and the logical,
Were bound in sonorous harmony.

Down in the inchoate cave of my heart,
In the *pension* in Lausanne long ago,
It was language,
Lovely French,
The surge and rush of words,
The slip, glide, roll of syllables,
That made manifest the saving stream of life
Running out of Eden and down through the ages,
That will pour at time's end into the Garden of God.

Fire on Riot Hill

Rough young men but kindly, they took
A liking to the lean lad from the East
Who worked with them in the mountains,
Trimming and settling to earth the scrub pine
And Ponderosa that the lumber-
Jacks knocked down but rejected
When they made their cut and took the big ones
For the sawmills in the Boise valley.

The house-lights dim, the curtain rises,
We're sitting in a circle on memory's stage

There's bull-necked Hank, who works
With weights and bench-presses every evening
In the bunk-house; his buddy, Earl
(A replica in miniature),
Sharp-tongued and cocky; quiet, earnest
Danny; Jim, big-boned and freckly,
With shovel-scoop hands that drag
The breakfast table every morning, raking up
Eggs and bacon, flapjacks, spuds;
And Gene, Indian-blooded, tireless, swift,
Who, like wind, loped past me once
When we were fighting a hill fire,
I lying pinned to earth, out for the count,
Bludgeoned by the choking smoke and heat.

FIRE ON RIOT HILL

In the woods each day our crew-boss,
Gnarled Old Bill, who has tiny feet and limps,
Keeps a squinty eye out on his boys
And sways among the toppled trees, flicking
His axe at the spoke-like, spiky
Branches like a boxer throwing jabs.
We crawl around the mountains, slashing and sawing,
And at noon crumple in the burning shade.

In August forest fires flare
All over the dried-out Sawtooth Range.
Yellow modulates to red.
Dozens of crews are called out to battle
The conflagration on Riot Hill,
Ignited by an arsonist's match.
We lay down a trench on the east slope to hold
The flames: in vain: they leap the width
And race toward the wooded summit,
Propagating westward and south. The whole
Hill soon is burning like a pyre,
A hundred acres of evergreen howling
To heaven, their needles exploding
As flame-bombs, wind-borne,
Boom in their tops and sizzle down the branches,
Girdling the clove-brown bark with red.

We watch Riot Hill from the facing
Slope, our mission to prevent the flames
From fanning eastward. A creek in the gulch

FIRE ON RIOT HILL

Between the hills is a natural break. Planes
Saturate the mountain with powder.
Trees burn. The charred woods weep and wail.
The Hill bakes. Roiling smoke caps
The upper slopes like piles of mushrooms.

The sun goes down in a monstrous blaze.
Clear, cold, black night steals on the hills.
We kindle some logs to keep warm.
Our campfire is life; the fire on the mountain,
Death. Flame-columns writhe on the Hill,
As if barbarians had put
The torch to a great cathedral. The abyss
Of night burns with a billion stars.

The V-shaped gulch, joined by the creek,
Rises to a closed ravine a half-mile off,
Where south and east slopes meet and the steep
Ridge running southward from Riot Hill
Blocks the gorge like a chimney wall.
To the underbrush and dense growth
At the foot of the Hill, burning spars
And severed limbs come tumbling down,
Lopped off by flame. In the center
Of the darkness the gulch is a furnace where ghouls
And fallen angels bleat like goats
And copulate convulsively with death.
At the campfire half a mile away,
Curled near the embers, I shudder

FIRE ON RIOT HILL

In troubled sleep: Troy, Rome, Dresden,
Hiroshima: Hell's apocalypse.

Morning is a gray desert, sullen.
Riot Hill is ash, punctured by the quills
Of blackened cedar, Ponderosa,
Naked Douglas fir. We tramp all day
Through the skeletal forest, wading
In cinders, stamping out hot spots,
Watering smoldering roots. Bones.
Smoke. Ghosts. Silence. World's end.

Fire has purged the great cathedral.
Do you recall what was written of old?
"Judgment begins in the House of God."
Howl, God-mockers! Weep, dissemblers!
Pillars of papier-mâché—how you have fallen!
The straight trees still stand, thick-barked
Towering trunks: but their needles are stripped,
Their vestments have gone up in flames.

"So you shall know that I am God."

Hank, Earl, Danny, Gene, Jim, Old Bill
And I, half-buried in ash, streaked black,
Slog over Riot Hill three long days,
Charcoal shades among the fuming dead,
Till relief comes and we return
To life, changed, saved out of fire.

FIRE ON RIOT HILL

All that happened long ago

Hank, have you kept fit since then?
Are your muscles tight? And you, Earl: who won,
Your tongue or your heart? Is your wife
Happy, Danny? Do you still eat for three,
Jim? And Gene—the cougar!—do you
Still lope like wind? Old Bill—I know
Your feet no longer walk those piney hills:
You're climbing happier mountains now.

As for me, well, I've gone through
Many fires since Riot Hill. You might not
Know me. I'm the same and not the same.
The fires have done it: fierce passion-flames,
Scorching the mind; blazes of orange
Violence; underground guilt-fires,
Riddling the weak heart; God-sent strikes
Of lightning aimed to purge the soul's
Dead wood and scatter hidden snakes.
I've suffered Love's fire, too, where the world
Turns cinnabar and drowns in heat
Until the flushed heart longs to be all lost,
All found! Do you hear me, companions
Of the wild hills? Peace be with us all!
May we meet at the End on the Mountain of God,
In the Fire of Christ's Blessed Kingdom!

FIRE ON RIOT HILL

The stage dims, the curtain falls,
The lights in the house come up.
I shake my head and look around.
Where am I?
Who are these people clapping?
Was it I tramped those hills?
Battled that fire?
In what age? What world?
Do I dream?
"It's time to go home," says a voice
In the empty theatre. "The play's over."

Today

How is it this past is present?
The heart aches—near breaks—to find my father right here
coming in from the fields at noon at the summons
of my English stepmother's gong, made by her father,
and he and Al and Dave and Johnny and the other Dave and I,
our stomachs scratched by hay, heads drooping under heat,
each pulling a soft drink from the cold water of the little creek
in the shadows under the log bridge—and the ecstasy,
as we sprawl on the logs, our bodies played out,
of the long cold deep drafts of orange, grape, or cream soda,
after hours hauling hay in the oven of summer.

And now Eve greets us, and her sandwiches and peas and pies,
my father's "yellow rose of England", blond as butter,
blue-eyed, proud of her men, aglow with the vigor
of the North she loves—the wild, dangerous, spruce-clad,
lonely North, maker and breaker of men.
Here Eve stands by the cabin door and greets us, the sweaty six,
coming up from the hayfields hungry and lean.

And we sit down and eat.

My father tells Eve how the clover is ripe and the windrows thick
and the slew grass in the meadow beyond the willows, up to his waist;
how the great red Massy Harris tractor turned on a dime,
and the yellow baler, pride of his life, banged out bales
all morning long, clearing the field. The smallest details
assume mythical proportions as he talks. At dessert he takes out

TODAY

his false teeth and makes funny faces till we're limp with laughter
(a wrench had knocked out seven teeth once when he was working under a tractor,
then a fly-by-night dentist had yanked out the rest),
while Eve chuckles and admires us all and serves up cherry pie.
Coffee time, he rolls a smoke, we sit around the table quiet,
resting, sobered, lost in a of haze of contentment, out of time,
till the moment comes and we rise and plod back to the fields.

This was not long ago, this was fifty years ago,
it wasn't even yesterday it happened, it is happening today.

My father and Eve left the North years later, they made a new life
    in Virginia.
The seasons turned, my father's strong frame shrunk,
the body of his "yellow rose" bent double.
The two grew old together and died a year apart;
now they are nowhere to be found on the earth,
neither in the North nor in Virginia nor anywhere else.
They are with God, extolling his creation, telling him
about the beauty of the mountains they've seen,
the great oceans and rivers and deep woods,
and the animals like moose and porcupine and lynx,
and the vegetables like spinach and peas and yellow squash.
The North—pearl of their hearts—glimmers like a distant star.

yet it is *now*, not once upon a time

the lunch-gong echoes over the fields long ago
now

TODAY

the creek purls beside us, bending the willows
we gulp down our soft drinks, orange, grape, cream
flat on our backs we stare up at infinity
blue
flowers near the outhouse
asters
blue
asters
we doze
blue cool creek cool breezes pale blue
the creek purls beside us cool
blue
we dream in the heat we rise walk from the bridge to the house
Eve greets us
we wash our hands in the tin tub and take our places at table
my father tells tall tales about how it was that morning in the hayfields
the ryegrass over our heads
we six all giants tossing huge bales
the yellow rose of England smiles at her silly men
my father makes funny faces and takes out his teeth
we laugh and laugh
Eve laughs

It is noon
once

TODAY

That moment in the history of the world wasn't yesterday
that moment is today
now

forever

Butterfly

I

Flitflitflit goes the butterfly,
Up/down, here/there,
Fluttering all over the place,
Staggering like a drunk:
Flitflitflit.
But the yellow butterfly is not a drunk:
It's a triangle of air made into a yellow solid
That weighs almost nothing
And bounces around among bushes like a rubber ball.
It flutters, flits,
Settles on a flower,
Sits,
Draws nectar,
Whisks to a lavender bush nearby,
Settles,
Imbibes,
Hops to a marjoram plant,
To a cardamom plant,
Skews to a thyme patch,
To the clusters of purple wisteria bedecking the wall,
To the wild rose by the gate,
The odoriferous sage near the water-tap,
The sharp-smelling mint in the earthenware pot:
Crazy!
The yellow butterfly is like a drunk reeling from bar to bar swilling beer.

But the butterfly is not a drunk—
It's a butterfly,
A yellow butterfly.

II

The butterfly flits through air
Like memory through time.
Its shadow on a wall,
Its reflection in a puddle,
Conjure the butterfly;
But they are *not* the butterfly,
No more than a memory of what once was
Is what once was.
Yet what is swaddled in time past,
Memory makes present,
As the butterfly's reflection conjures the creature.

III

I hear a melody lifting from a yellow field
Sprinkled with hay bales.
I'm a young boy on a tractor with my father.
"Chuck-a-luck, luck-luck, chuck-a-luck, luck-luck",
Goes the baler.
I see my father at the wheel,
Chiseled features,
Strong.
I jump off at a stook to load bales on the hay-rick,

Then jump up again.
The sun is hot,
The air full of straw.
I grip my father's shoulder,
His hands grip the wheel.
"Good job, son."

Joy

Once is now

The melody suddenly ceases

    IV

An ache overcomes me.
Oh, *loss*!
Yet the ache points forward,
Not only backward.
It points over mountains, forests, cities,
It points over years, over lives,
It pierces through memories.
"You will hear the melody again," the ache says.
"Beyond time.
The melody is love."

Memory, You are Cruel

Memory, you are cruel. When the sun's ray
Wakes us from welcome slumber, and gone-by years
Lift from Lethe to mock our forlorn day,
Illness closing off new common pleasures
And few prospects beckoning in the threadbare hours,
Then images of once-upon-a-time invade
The mind, and you make once bright flowers
Bloom again in the heart, quickly to fade.
Thus, memory, all your echoing melodies
Played once with energy and verve
Sound again—briefly!—then turn to threnodies
For lack of a weight on time's scales to serve
A genial future—then no loyal friend
Are you, but cruel soothsayer of our end.

A Prayer

Illuminate my shadows, Lord.
Against these sheets of dark that set
Sharp shapes across my walls, send a sword
Of light; on these shards of debt
Pass your stain-removing blood,
As, to illuminate a plain,
You might part clouds, let gold sun flood
The land, drown the dark, then drain
Away the shadow from our sight.
Illuminate my shadows, Lord.
Where loneliness still spreads fright
Inside my soul, speak your kind word.
Be my friend, Lord. In silence take
My hand, be my companion. I shiver
Sometimes in the cold night. Shake
Off my fears, Belovéd. Sever
Me from the blight of our bleak
Age, make me joyous. You are joy,
Lord. Love. Our great Father. You seek
Me as I seek you. Oh, destroy
In me self-doubt, cruel worm that eats
The heart.
   When we *serve*, it shrivels.
Doubt goes. Blithe service soon defeats
The sullen canker, quickens verve.
In you, Savior, I meet the Other;
I meet my friends, my most dear wife,
Enemies, the wounded. You smother

A PRAYER

Anxious, bleating self. You give life,
Lord. Yours. It's *your* life you offer.
You strap my shadows to your chest,
Then plunge into night. As you suffer,
They die. Praise God! O Lord,
Number me among the blest.

The Bell

It will be time soon to round the corner
At the end of the avenue I know so well.
Time to leave old haunts, not as mourner,
Nor weeping, but as one who hears the bell
Tolling: "Wake, wake!", and chimes ringing
Changes in the tower of the ancient cathedral
Built once in drained swampland by singing
Servants of God. "Wake!" it tolls. "Revel
In the light springing up in the East, at the end
Of the tortuous road where raucous crowds
Howl. Wake from sleep! The time's come round
To throw off tatters and night's soiled shrouds!"
Oh, heart, wake! Rise! Let hope swell!
Hear Christ's chimes ringing old earth's knell!

Part V

The Stallion

I cannot say I'm perfectly at rest.
I've been ploughed, disced, harrowed,
My soil has been sliced,
It is tender, it hurts.
But I tell myself:
Ploughed sods also *shine*;
And disc and harrow *prepare soil for seed*.
So really I should be perfectly at rest,
Like the wasp on the window pane near me,
Preening its wings the way ducks do;
Or like the white cat on the garden wall,
Bathing blithely in the shadows of branches.

I've been riding a stallion for years,
A stallion called faith;
The reins are called hope.
A powerful stallion, muscles rippling,
Its flesh and sweat stinging my nostrils.
The reins guide it well—but what terrain!
Woods, fields, marshes, mountain passes,
Streams to ford,
Rivers to swim,
Gorges to be threaded like needles.
But the stallion hasn't faltered,
The reins haven't dropped from my hands.
I've hung on.

THE STALLION

And the stallion knows where it is going,
It is following its Master.

So I should be perfectly at rest, should I not?

Night-Hawk

O night, you drop dark-wingèd down
Out of speckled black space, hawk-like;
You plunge earthward to seize me,
Seize poor rabbit,
Rabbit in the desert, lost, streaking,
Ears in flight, flat,
Eyes moons fear-filled,
Rabbit out there where no shelter is,
By the night-hawk targeted—
Oh poor rabbit, bounding now,
Fur straight up, star-lit,
The hawk's dive sensed,
Rabbit in the cross-hairs—
How escape?
How escape night's plunge,
The hawk's devouring mouth?

Yet now in night's very throat a star stands forth,
In the black it blazes,
Bursts,
Spews out its matter,
Dies,
Supernova seeding space—
And I, rabbit,
Nearly night's prey,
Nearly caught—
Am caught . . . *up*!
Am by Light loosed from black,

NIGHT-HAWK

Snatched from the night-hawk's claws—
I, rabbit, saved!
By the star's burst—saved!

And it is the hawk who is doomed—
Old Night—
Shredded by a Star.

A Vision

The shadow of the smoke from the chimney
Slithers like a grass snake over the wall and up the slope.
Sun melts the icing on the chocolate hill.
A toy car zigzags down the road from the hilltop.
Blue invades the air like a tide.
Morning! Motion!
Night's ghouls slink down into subconscious caves.
Shards of broken glass in my brain assemble into window panes.
Light swells.
Out of gloom grow forms,
Inside gaps grow shapes.
What were fumes in night's coils become scents.

I *see*!
I see pansies in pots on the porch.
I see houses with wide-open shutters and orange-tiled roofs.
Far off at the edge of the sky I see mountains,
Their slopes white like angels' wings.
Trees hemming their skirts are like writing on a parchment:
"*I give you a hope and a future.*"
My God!
The tips of my fingers set to tingling,
My feet set to tapping,
My legs dance,
My heart beats like a drum—
Life!

Her Dear Face

Shall I soon welcome back again my love?
Shall her dear face, like the gentle moon,
Shine mellow once again in our old home
And generate,
As might a wood stove burning maple logs,
Warmth in its cold rooms,
Life again where loss had made a tomb?

Mouse

Mouse peeks out of a hole.
It is *hope*.
It twitches its nose,
Sensing my presence.
Its bright black eyes say:
"Hello! I'm Mouse. I'm *hope*.
I live in a hole,
But here I am,
I've come out into broad daylight.
Don't chase me away.
Let me poke around your kitchen
And find crumbs to eat:
On your table,
Under your chair,
In your cupboard.
You have lots of crumbs I can eat.
Let me eat them.
You've scared me away recently,
You've been fretting
And making lots of noise.
But here I am,
I'm not going to be afraid.
I don't want you to be afraid either.
My name is Mouse.
I'm *hope*.
Welcome me."

Scribbles

My brain scribbles on the blackboard of night.
It's scarily dark outside.
The moon is hidden.
The chalk of my brain screeches unpleasantly.

Out on the cosmic tundra
A dog yaps.
Yapyap.
Yap.
No answer.
Yap.
It's as though a star way off nowhere set to barking.
Yap.
Yapyap.

I scribble and scribble

It is cold.

Suddenly the backlit clouds covering the moon—
Which have the look of rumpled sheets where lovers lay—
Part.
And lo, there sits the moon like an egg in a nest of cloud
And stars are popping up all over the place
To pay homage,
To admire,
Or simply to gaze with wonder upon the moon-egg.

SCRIBBLES

Who laid it?

I can't scribble fast enough

When I was a boy I gathered eggs in a henhouse.
That was a very long time ago
And as far away
As the lonely dog-yaps on the tundra of night.
Time has gobbled up those eggs.
Time gobbles up everything.

Scribblescribble

Hold on—not so fast!
Those eggs are still in my brain,
They're here on the blackboard!

Scribble

As the moon-egg in its nest of rumpled sheets speaks of love,
So the eggs in my brain speak of spirit.

Scribblescribble

My neurons are matter,
Yes,
But they generate immaterial museums,
Museums that signal,
In the manner of a figure,

SCRIBBLES

A different kind of museum from what we know on earth—
A museum where all the displays—
Like "memories", if you will—
Are like spiritual bodies full of life.
They are what they once were
And they are not what they once were.
They are alive—
But differently,
Incorruptibly.
They have been transformed.

Scribblescribblescribble

No question here of inert objects,
Of objects gobbled up by time.

Is this not a figure of eternity,
Of Life in the Kingdom of God?

Scribblescribblescribblescribble

www.ingramcontent.com/pod-product-compliance
Lightning Source LLC
LaVergne TN
LVHW051657080426
835511LV00017B/2612